# Angels

## Ronan O'Donnell

First performed at 'A Play, a Pie and a Pint',
Òran Mór, Glasgow 12–17 September 2011
Traverse Theatre, Edinburgh 2–26 August 2012

# Angels

## by Ronan O'Donnell

| | |
|---|---|
| NICK PRENTICE | **Iain Robertson** |

| | |
|---|---|
| Director | **Graeme Maley** |
| Music | **Benedikt Hermann Hermannsson** |
| Press & Marketing | **Sarah Findlay** |
| Company Manager | **Irvine Allan** |
| Original Photo | **Nobby Clark** |
| Art Design | **Jóhanna Helga www.johannahelga.com** |

### Thanks

Blindhorse would like to thank David MacLennan.

Special thanks also to Producer-mentor
Lalitha Rajan.

Our web site www.blindhorse.co.uk was built and designed
by Seweryn Siewert. (http://eswues.info/contact)

Thanks also to Dani Rae, Steven Mabbot, Sam Pilling,
Bill Dunlop  Henry Adam, Iain MacArthur of Jewel & Esk
College, Chris Horricks and Remarkable Television.

*Blindhorse*

www.blindhorse.co.uk

# COMPANY

**Iain Robertson –** NICK PRENTICE
Iain Robertson trained at the Sylvia Young Theatre
School.

Theatre credits include: *My Romantic History*
(Traverse, Edinburgh/Bush, London); *Confessions of a
Justified Sinner* (Royal Lyceum, Edinburgh); *Small
Craft Warnings* (Arcola, London); *Romeo and Juliet,
Blood Wedding* (Citizens, Glasgow); *Strangers,
Babies, The Slab Boys Trilogy* (Traverse, Edinburgh);
*The Tempest* (Old Vic/Sheffield Crucible); *Passing
Places* (Greenwich, London); *The Good Hope, The
Winter's Tale, The Mysteries* (National Theatre).

Film and television credits include: *Acts of Godfrey,
Rab C. Nesbitt, Next Time Ned, The Contractor, Basic
Instinct 2, Casualty, Sea of Souls, One Last Chance,
Gunpowder, Treason & Plot, Taggart, Band of
Brothers, Watchmen, Hereafter, Fat Chance,
Homesick, Oliver Twist, Rebus, Poached, Grange Hill,
Plunkett & Macleane, The Match, The Debt
Collector, Bramwell, Psychos, Trial by Jury, The Bill,
Silent Witness, A Mug's Game, Bodyguards, Small
Faces, Kavanagh QC.*

Radio credits include: *McLevy: The Blue Gown, An
Audience with Ed Reardon, The Sensitive, My Blue
Hen, The Astronaut, Tough Love, Jimmy Murphy
Makes Amends, Rebus – Black and Blue, Saturday,
Sunday, Monday, The Tenderness of Wolves, Faust,
The Best Snow for Skiing, Japanese Tales, Soft Fall the
Sounds of Eden, Just Prose, The Nativity, The Passion,
The Prisoner of Papa Stour.*

**Ronan O'Donnell** – Writer
Ronan O'Donnell lives in Edinburgh.

Theatre credits include: *The Doll Tower* (Unity Theatre); *Spambam* (LookOut Theatre Company); *Brazil* (Arches, Theatre of Imagination); *The Chic Nerds* (Traverse, Edinburgh). In 2004, he was involved in the translation and writing of a new version of Wang Xiaoli's *In the Bag*, the first production of a contemporary play from mainland China, for the Traverse.

**Graeme Maley** – Director
Maley's recent directing and developing credits include: *And The Children Never Looked Back* by Salka Gudmundsdottir; *Angels* by Ronan O'Donnell, (Òran Mór); *Djupid* (The Deep) by Jón Atli Jónasson, (Òran Mór/Assembly, Edinburgh); *Ten Days on the Island* (Tasmania); *The Track of the Cat* by Chris Fittock and Graeme Maley (Eugene O'Neill Foundation, San Francisco/Reno Little Theatre, Nevada). He is currently writing and directing a community show in Royston, Glasgow.

**Benedikt Hermann Hermannsson** – Music

Benedikt is a composer from Iceland. He leads the band Benni Hemm Hemm. Benni Hemm Hemm varies in size and style containing from one to forty members. Sometimes it is a full orchestra with huge brass and string sections, sometimes it's a six-piece pop band and sometimes it is a solo singer/songwriter-style performance. All contain singer and multi-instrumentalist Benedikt H. Hermannsson playing his songs and arrangements.

Before starting the project Benni Hemm Hemm, Benedikit was in the bands Rúnk and Mósaík with indie heavyweights Svavar Pétur Eysteinsson (of Skakkamanage and Prinspóló), Hildur Guðnadóttir (of múm), Ólafur Björn Ólafsson (of Yucatan and Jónsi) and Björn Kristjánsson (of Borko). In 2004 he called together a group of his friends to perform some of his songs and arrangements. The event was an instant success and soon they found themselves recording new songs in Sundlaugin, and making the self-titled debut LP, Benni Hemm Hemm.

Since then Benni Hemm Hemm has released six albums and the seventh is on the way. He has played hundreds of concerts and travelled across the USA, and performed in many cultural festivals around the world.

He worked with director Graeme Maley on *Track of the Cat* at the 2010 Edinburgh Festival Fringe, performing his music live. This 2012 Edinburgh Fringe Festival he has composed music for Molly Taylor's *Love Letters to the Public Transport System* for the National Theatre of Scotland at the Assembly Rooms.

For more info on Benni and his music go to www.bennihemmhemm.com

**Sarah Findlay** – Press & Marketing
Hailing from Inverkeithing, Sarah graduated from Queen Margaret University in 2012 gaining a degree in Drama and Theatre Arts, specialising in Arts Journalism. At university she took a particular interest in feminism and Scottish theatre with an emphasis on the work of playwright Rona Munro. For the last few years Sarah has written for the online arts and entertainment outfit Tvbomb, reviewing, previewing and writing features during the Edinburgh Fringe Festival, Edinburgh International Festival and Edinburgh Film Festival, and providing year round coverage of the art scene in Glasgow and Edinburgh.

**Irvine Allan** – Company Manager
Irvine lectures in Drama and Performance at Queen Margaret University. His career spans both film and theatre. He was a founder member and director of the highly acclaimed Cat. A. Theatre Company. For many years the company toured venues in Scotland and England with a special focus on prison drama. The company garnered a clutch of Fringe Firsts along the way, including awards for *No Mean Fighter* in 1992 and *Dirt Enters at the Heart* in 1994. Other notable successes were *Doing Bird* in 1995 and *Witch Doctor* in 1997.

Irvine founded Young Miracle Films, T/A Indelible Inc in 1999, after cutting his teeth in community and short-ilm making. In 2001 *Daddy's Girl* (BBC2 10x10) won the Cannes Institute's Film Festival Prix du Jury. *My Daughter's Face* (1999) won the Special Jury Award, Palm Springs IFF USA, among other accolades. He has currently three films in various stages of production.

He recently produced and directed Ronan O'Donnell's screenplay, *Daydream in the Honest Toun*, in association with Queen Margaret University.

Ronan and Irvine are currently developing another screenplay for Places for People Scotland, shooting in autumn 2012.

# INTRODUCTION

It's often asked who a playwright writes for? Does he write for himself totally or the ideal audience member? Is he morally neutral, as Graham Greene said somewhere – an observer and non-interventionist whose duty it is to stand by the swamp and watch thirstily as its victims struggle? But Greene was an author with a metaphysical universe within which his characters strive by faith for redemption or rage against God – 'that bastard', as the atheist called 'Him'. The striving and the rage are both acts of affirmation: a bit like Johnny Cash whose point of composition as a sinner enriches both his song and the sense we have of his personal journey.

A self-contained moral universe is a perfect medium for an author's inventions, where a character is the product of his inner self's emanations. Given the crisis of morality in all areas of our public life, moral perceptions may seem to be a communicative and political fallacy where, in the name of a dirty realism we must, like the blazered gaffers of the SFA, disown principle as a luxury commodity. But I'd argue we are of necessity moral engineers and the chief engineer sits with his calculus in the centre of our DNA. Morality or collective ethics is a cultural pattern that by the necessity of happiness is a form of collective dream as old and older than the rocky grottos where aboriginal storytellers painted the plot of their origins. The theatre is the stylisation of that 'divine dream' that prompts actions in the outer world and which requires its audience to experience and collude in its fictive truths. The author may be conflicted in his personal morality but by the act of writing he becomes a kind of moral agent.

The inner necessities that drive human motive form an old family group in perpetual discord. Pulling them together for the duration of the play and getting them to sing from the same hymn sheet for a wee bit is one of the playwright's jobs. If the writer only wrote for himself, it would be like George Best taking his ball into the woods to do the keepy-ups and dribbles by himself, and ultimately where's the fun and the play in that?

> *Brush ma shodder wi yer wand o magic*
> *Glitter instances wi buzz an astonished gawks*
> *Kiss the auld yin's cheek wi tear an treasure*
> *Nae mawkin-mad mawkin-fly pester*
> *Dip the nib o yer master-pen*
> *In the well o yer marra*
> *Swoop wi swifts*
> *Stab like gannet in yer wave an welter*
> *Laughter tae wit cries the ways o man*
> *An wumman an aw*
> *In the cave o sorrow light yer connell*
> *Aware that sanctimony has easy lines and smells –*
> *Jester o a anvil an a hammer*
> *Jester in a glass space-suit*
> *Moon walks roond aboot the planet Plautus*
> *Wi a wean's  jinkie giggle*
> *Wi a wean's grab at the apple.*

*Ronan O'Donnell*

'O´Donnell writes for no one. Not a theatre, and certainly not a producer, director or dramturgically-led literary department. O´Donnell´s only obligation is to his voice and use of language. *Angels* is an emphatic example of the originality and power this methodology creates.'

*Graeme Maley,*
*July 2012*

# ANGELS

Ronan O'Donnell

*For Jenny Sheldon*

*This text went to press before the end of rehearsals and so may differ slightly from the play as performed.*

NICK PRENTICE, *thirty-one, in a small interview room in a police station. He works as a security guard and is wearing the company shirt, black trousers and no shoes. The only set is the fluorescent light tube in the ceiling.*

## One

Interview room's tiny – way overheated, bit of a jannie's kip hole under the school boiler room – no windows just a long tube o neon leaking its light from behind a security grill. Now an again the neon fizzes – erratically blinks – snap, dork, snap! I adjust my eyes. Here, time crawls backwards into its fossily shell. But I feel grateful for that. Not sure why. Maybe it's like the interval between blows. It's no like anybody has hit me yet, but you would value greatly the interval between blows, wouldn't you? You would value tiny inconsequential routines in a room like this and wrap the grey stretch about you like an auld stale blanket. Check this oot – it's boiling hot but my hands are shaking. I looks about me for the first time. The walls are covered in excremental slogans. Underpass graffiti. A forest o cocks and balls o various sizes with tears of spurting cum. You wonder at the ingenuity since the writings are scratched and gouged and wrote in smoke, an the ceiling too is covered in tags and wit look like Banksy-inspired stencils o venomous monkeys. Gurning baboon faces peering through the swastikas. The room has a smack and smell all o its own – It's like keekin through a loom o smoke although there's a large no-smoking sign on the wall in front o me and I canny imagine the rules being flaunted willy-nilly round here – I'm gasping for a fag. I can smell the golden toasty fumes. Oh, for the crinkly plastic wrapping an the swan-white fag papers an the horsehair snout. The fumbled rolling an ritual o a single-skinner. But for all its uncared-for grime I know I'm in a room o iron protocol. No smoking. It's as if the graffiti is aw that's left wance the

shouting an bawling has been drained away. And in regard to
this room the graffiti's akin to the red-velvet upholstery o a
theatre box at the King's, part o the essential decor o the place.
A perfect room to put the boot in. It's a room that forgets wit
folk here hae endured. A shift in my seat and I can feel a bead
of sweat running down the base of my spine into the gully
between the cheeks o ma arse. My solicitor provided by the
station authorities sits next to me at the metal table and is
leaning his shoulder again the wall, checking his fingernails.
This is as far away as he can get frae me whilst still sitting next
tae me. Perfunctory grunts, a clammy handshake and then stum.
I, for the life of me, couldny LEGO a question together to ask
my learned pal. I opened my mouth to try a couple of times but
couldn't frame or even think o a relevant query, which in truth's
but a vain attempt to establish my presence as a personage o
gritty depth and breezy wit. But the words were glue on my
tongue and come out as gummy grumbles which he examined
frae behind the double glazing o his specs, but briefly and wi
the air o a grudge. A left him to his cuticles – focused on a fly
buzzing the no-smoking sign. Frae a pipe that climbed a corner
an disappeared into the ceiling came crunkly wheezes and
distant air-trapped gurgles. Then a tingle o excitement frae us
both as the door is unbolted and the inspector's let in. The
door's quickly shut behind him like tae keep the public safe frae
a noxious danger. Me or the brief? The brief he's sharpening a
pencil. The inspector takes a couple o steps into the room,
filling his lungs wi air, and boldly cracks a file onto the table in
front o me. Still stonnin he looks me up and down in a right
brazen way. His nostrils flared like he's stood in puddle o piss.
He himsel smelt o knocked-off aftershave. There was no
allegiance to a brand here, but the hurried ablutions o a minor
official trying to cover up the wild-garlic smell o his lonely
wanks. He never says anything – then after a while o me
shufflin in ma seat he says, letting oot his intake o breath, he
says: 'So tell me in your own words what actually happened,
sonny?' He was examining a mustardy stain on his tie when he
says this, so I'm puzzled as to who this deceptively casual
interrogation is addressed to. It floats in the air like the ghost o a
butterfly you ken yi'll never catch or see again. My mouth

hangs slack as I contemplate the mental moth smoke and trace its raj loops. The lawyer geez me a nudge. Then another sharper nudge, 'One moment he was standing there, the next he was falling.' I let out the sentence in a squeaky spasm an I'm quite surprised wi its accuracy. The inspector seemed please wi this statement an scrunted his crutch like he was putting the Volvo in gear, then he drew the chair oot on his side o the desk so the legs scraped the bare concrete floor and he did it like he wanted to seed that sound in ma napper and then having done that he quite casually planks his arse. He seemed much irritated by the mustard smug on his tie and kept returning to it with smouldering ire. 'Noo,' he says, 'we can dae this the easy way or the hard way.' He opens the palms of his hands like he's showing me a glass melon: 'It's up to you, sonny.' My brief coughed like he's reminding the inspector o his presence in the room. The inspector leaned o'er and switched tape recorder on.

How to put into words the fact he was laughing as he fell from the concrete parapet to his death, and how to tell what I felt his wild laughter meant as he tumbled through the air. Laughter that came to a sudden end wi a smash-the-chocolate-easter-egg crunch. I couldn't say that. Couldn't find the words wit his laughin… And I was good with words an aw. In the boom years of the late nineties no one sold more mobile phones than me. A even chatted up Harry Carpenter when he called to register. A commercial indiscretion that had, wi ma pals, long lost its fizz.

The room bulges wi silence. The inspector interprets my inner ambivalence wi expert ease. 'Would it be easier if you wrote it down, sonny,' he sort o sneered. 'You like writing don't you.' How'd he know… 'Found this in your room.' He opens the file on the table real slow like he's Sherlock Holmes revealing the last bit o jigsaw that proves the case and slaps a pile of paper onto the desk in front of me. 'Prima facie,' he says oot loud, 'Prima facie,' declares it to the four walls as if looking for a respondee frae among the forest o graffiti. I look around myself to see where a reply might come frae. 'Prima facie,' ma lawyer beside me sighs like the inspector's nabbed a spanner that rightly belongs in his toolbox. 'Well,' the inspector blow-dries intae ma face his beery breath, 'hae yi anything tae say for yerself, sonny?' Then he says tae ma brief about me: 'Bit o a bachelor's son if you catch ma drift.'

Bewilderment fugs ma brain as I try to take in the morning's swirling happenings. Under the table my leg's vibrating an a stub the heel o wan foot into the toes o the other to damp the shaking doon – A bit o self-inflicted pain to induce some control. I surmise the inspector has been in ma room. Checked under the mattress an went rifling through ma drawers – so to speak. Been round about ma trainers and thumbled in my plastic bag fu o odd socks. Laughed at my meagre porn collection. Laughed at the solitary suit hanging in ma wardrobe, laughed at the Aldi label. An he's got in his mitts my secret writing no for awbudie's eyes but mine. Is there no privacy laws in this fuckin country? He's obviously read ma wee fantasy story. A blush an my lugs radiate a caught-red-handit glow. A felt like A've been stripped naked an made to wear a pair o high heels and sent totterin doon a vast corridor lined wi iron studded doors wi Judas peepholes. I instinctively cupped ma knackers. Then my hands flashed to my heed and I found mysel sort o running my fingers through ma hair an a felt a smile o cracked nonchalance dribble across ma mug. The neon snapped like wan o they Venus flytraps. Zzzzz snap, snap… snap. An in the dork the purple outline o the inspector swam for a few seconds behind my eyelids. Dragon purple like A was in a fuckin David Icke nightmare.

He stabbed the pile o A4 wi his fat finger. '*Angels* it's called. Nothing to do with angels at all.' He wore his gold sovereigns like knuckle dusters. 'Oh I know what your solicitor's going to say: "Isn't relevant!" But I think it is, isn't it? Shows his moral character in a blistering light if you ask me. Corroborating evidence.' Ma brief sneers at a bit o station grime under his thumbnail. Then tuts as the over-sharp nib o his pencil breaks first time when he presses it to a piece o blank paper. The inspector folds his arms and leans back in his chair. The sort of inspector he is who thinks, 'At your age I was flying choppers in the Falklands! Fuckin dodgin Exocet missiles an slottin Argies on Tumbledown. This generation o deadbeats deserve to be hounded. If A could I'd tak extraordinary measures an A'd use them wi relish on the verminy neds' – I could see that was what was in his bullish head as he scratched the mustardy stain on his tie wioot lookin at it. I thought I could see a growing intemperance in every movement of his body an to deflect the imminent eruption A frankly stammered the start o various admissions. I'd clear his books! That's the perverse thought that zipped through ma bonce – just dinny hit me. No the face. A charcoaled wad o sins and wrongdoing welled up frae some unkent tunnel deep in ma chest but there was a bottleneck in my throat an a spaghetti junction wioot an exit ramp in my nut. An A glabbered mixty-maxty bullshit but the reek o guilt was evident to the professionals present in this horribly shrinking room. I feel myself shrinking visibly, ma claiths suddenly too big for me. My socks slid doon my shins an hung about my ankles.

A silent air of glee and puffed-up conviction at ma visible wilting is shared by the inspector an ma brief, then after a wee cough the inspector admitted a tiny social deficiency and produced a pair o bifocals which he put on. Did it like no one was supposed to notice. He pushes a pen an blank paper towards me and withoot a word awaited the inevitable scrawl. Confession time dinged I guess. I lifted the grubby pen and swallows hard – it, the pen, felt like it was a link in the chain of my destiny. I could have wept at the weight, the substance of the thing and it a mere BIC. If he wants a confession I'd gee him wan. Disorientated eh? Gasping for a fag. You'd confess tae anything.

While I'm wrestling wi where to start the inspector slides a page o *Angels* over to my brief, who nibbled it up wi eager fingers. It seems in investigating one alleged crime they had uncovered a mouldering nest of various infamies – ma wee porn story being chief among the corroborating articles. They might as well have found a balaclava hanging up tae dry er ma sink. Night-vision goggles an pink fluffy cuffs. The hale night attire o a Niddrie knicker- thief. Forgive me, Scarlett – I had not meant ma private smitten ramblings to be aired in such a place as this. The inspector tapped the A4 pile as my brief read a random extract o *Angels* wi a look o fascination mixed wi flabbargastit horror. Dread like a pair o shades in a suddenly dark an silent nightclub clouded my wonky vision and the blank page the inspector presented me wi swam in and out o focus. I hovered wi ma BIC but the thing I had to write doon was intricate and amorphous like the vale concealing some beauty in a dream I couldny jerk aside. Just then in a piece o cosmic synchronicity ma brief in a gasp read aloud, 'Scarlett Johansson walked in naked wi her snowy breasts, each one snug in a champagne glass which she held so to obscure blue shadowed nipples.' The inspector promptly stopped scratching the mustard stain on his tie an half-rose oot his seat. 'Wit the fuck...' he mutters. 'I missed that bit.'

I stuck my head doon an focused on the blank page in front of me, expecting a sharp blow aboot my lug but like A says I was at a loss where to start – my hand started to tremble again – mouth turns dry. For I'd been brought in for questioning some hours ago, lifted at my work in front of aghast colleagues and as yet no one had bothered to inform me of a charge or what exactly was the crime I was suspected of. I looked from the inspector to my brief in some bewilderment but they offered no clues as to my transgression, if any. Both now seems put oot by the delay in my spilling the beans and the delay was lengthened by a welling of self-pitying tears that blurs my eyes. But I knew I wasny innocent. I knew it would be terrible to sit here as a totally innocent man. Such a state would prevent acclimatisation and undermine morale entirely. But all the same it was horrible to think I could get used to this place and its rhythms. A high-pitched wheeze came frae the pipe in the corner and I allowed myself to ponder its significance. Get on wi it, nudges ma brief, as he reaches for another page o *Angels* to read. All I could do was look at the blank paper in front o me, the BIC frozen in my haund.

He stood there on the concrete parapet and before he sort o fell into the arms o gravity, before he leaned back he started to laugh. Somehow the pen in my hand wouldn't budge, wouldn't or couldn't find the words to describe what happened to Gary Glover. At this lengthening delay the inspector was first disconsolate an my brief offered him an assuaging mint but he refused it like he wanted salt no sugar on his holy porridge, like he was martyred by the halt in proceedings and then he rose

slowly to his feet an after a glance at the mustard stain, from a
hideously deep trouser pocket the inspector drew his truncheon
and slammed it on the desk. Whack! Whack and then again
whack! Like he was trying tae milk the ink frae ma file. Whack,
whack an whack he bludgeoned mercilessly that sorry wee porn
story called *Angels*! I knew noo why the table was made o
metal. What a fuckin battering he gave those pages and it was
wi a mixture o relief an horror that A let out a shriek an looked
at my brief who was polishing his specs – an a thought zipped
through my trembling brain – the brief looks like Capello,
know, the England manager, grim in his hidden satisfactions.
Then the inspector was taking off his jacket like he meant to
engage in hefty labour, but in his rage he couldny quite get his
elbows through his sleeves and he roared and bellowed like the
thwarted Houdini o a madhouse until the brief wi some
decorum as if he'd often helped a loon oot a straitjacket
smoothly got the inspector's jacket off and even, you ken,
dusted it doon like a waiter wid a tuxedo. The inspector was
wearing wan o they polystyrene short-sleeved shirts wi pens
peepin oot the breast pocket. Yon cuntish brute thinks he's in
the LAPD. He raised his truncheon high er his heed but before
he can splatter ma parting he spots the brief like a disapproving
Fabio Capello on the sidelines shaking his heid. A can hear
someone shouting for water, water, a glass o water please. Am
thinking it's some poor soul in the next cell then I realise wi
inconsolable shock the dude shouting for water is me. The neon
light buzzes like it is frying a fly and A musta passed oot. A
woke up on the floor. Nae one in the room but me, the three
chairs and on the table a tall plastic glass o water. In it floated –
strange tae tell – a handful o petals frae a yellow rose an wan
dead bluebottle. I took a sip but before I slipped back into
unconsciousness I heard myself saying: 'I shall pray. I shall
pray.' An the pipe whined an bubbles glugs.

**Two**

I want to wake up cos am dreaming am in the middle o a lang
pish. Hot streaming strool o urine overflowing the sink in ma
away digs. Strinkling the walls an carpet – let strong waters
flow! An then the horrors – ma cock's stroopless, wioot a spout.
A thin rill o milk leaks, poor stroakings, poor strippings. Then a
dream… dream some mair. Dream – o a multi-decked concrete
car park – it's where A work an where I bring my flask of coffee.
A wind's blawin and although A canny feel the cold A zip up my
jacket to the neck an muffle ma lugs uner ma woolly hat. The
view from one side over the parapet is aw clang and boom. I
watch as huge mental jaws swoop down into vast holds scooping
out and dumping ores in pyramids on the jetty. On another ship,
steam frae hundreds of vents billows into night air. The top deck
of the seven-storey car park usually only has one or two cars this
time of night. Belonging to cleaners or late-working managerial
types. The car decks are attached at each level to a glittering
world of things to buy. I prefer my coffee break here cos the staff
rest room has no ventilation and is sponsored by talk about crap
football hate jocks. It's out the way and there's always
something to see below in the docks whilst puffing a sneaky cig.
This night is no different from the rest as I sip ma coffee and
wish for a poke o chips. Then I spot Gary Glover in the shadows
near the entrance to C&A. Wit's he doing here? He's waving his
arm, beckoning me over. I look up at the various cameras
covering level seven and see – he's standing in a blind spot not
covered by CCTV. He's holding his arms wide like he's inviting
a hug. This some sort o set-up? A curse the fact that am on ma
tod. I could do wi a credible witness when dealing wi Gary
Glover. He couldny tell his sharp suits stuck oot in the one-
pound shop. An then through the glass sliding doors behind him,
frae amongst the glamorous mannequins strides, in the buff,
Scarlett Johansson in a shift made o cigar smoke. A blue light fas
on her and she spangles like a fairy queen. Then she leans over

an kisses Glover on the cheek. Am gobsmacked. Scarlett
Johansson an him are pals. They go way back. You can tell the
way he paws her erms. They couldny hae gone tae school
together? She's no frae Broomhouse. She no frae Broomhouse.
That's what I keep telling myself. She's no frae Broomhouse.

## Three

'As shugley as a Broomhouse docot.' My old gran used to say
so when she was scrutinising my schoolboy alibis. 'As shugley
as a Broomhouse docot, son.' I can hear the inspector speaking
this as he shuffles some papers. Resting my head in my arms,
slumped on the table, coming out a deep snooze. I decide to
play possum, draw my horns in an cock ma lug. My brief and
the inspector are jousting in an argumentative but friendly
manner and my radar lugs tunes into their blethers. I quickly
learned I'd apparently written some sort of statement which was
news to me. Musta wrote it in my sleep. As you do.

'Ye see what he's scribed here?' the inspector's saying to ma
brief. 'Read it oot,' says he. 'He ripped her stockings in a
hopeless manner. She asked him to lip them an so his tongue
rasped the silk all the way up her calf and thigh to the white
wobbly flesh below her gusset. Stocking tastes o perfumed
metallica.' 'Aye, then, then cop for this bit,' 'The door opens
and Scarlett is joined by Ursula the chambermaid dressed as a
nun. The Mother Superior in kinky wimples.' – 'He's doing a
Max Mosley here if you ask me. All the eminent symbols
humanity holds dear effin smeared.' They guffawed an chortled
like schoolboys at that sharp comparison.

'My client has no right to incriminate himself,' says ma brief.
'That's for me to do.' A statement which pricked my lugs and
drew a low moan that was ignored.

The inspector shot back, 'It bothers me how your high-handed
profession always presumes some sort of moral waiver. It just

confuses people, if you ask me. They don't know what to believe. It's sharp practice, Alistair.'

'Dougal, Dougal,' says ma brief, 'It wouldn't be professional if there weren't some ethical deferment – morality might be the head of reason but in our profession like Walt Disney, it's been cryogenically suspended. Otherwise the wheels of justice would grind to a halt – adversarial skill is all.'

'What about the evidence? The facts speak for themselves.'

'The facts speak for themselves all right and they shout in rough accent from midst a thicket of weasel-interest,' snorted the lawyer.

'But Scots law rests on the power o corroboration.'

'What you call corroboration I regard as mere conjecture. The truth is there is no defence. That's what the years have taught me. You can quote me *obiter dictum*.'

'This is moral relativism, huh? – If all it comes down to is presentation and slick patter. As a detective I stand full square behind the facts. What's the point o the big whiteboard up in the office an linking daisy chains o dates an suspects. Facts, Alistair. Facts can't suffer death by PowerPoint. The truth will out.'

'A fact is an idol in a shrine of wishful thinking. Yes you can photograph it, collate it, give it a chronology and a legend *ex facie* – all are attempts to triangulate a vapour. Come down off your high horse, Inspector. Admit it. We're de facto Lansprisado.'

'I'm not familiar wi that piece o legal jargon – Lanskidado?'

'Broken lances, Dougal. Horsemen serving in the foot regiment is all we've amounted to.'

'I used to think you were a big U2 fan – when you went on about pro-Bono.' A cruel cynicism fanged their jibes now. Like mates on the golf course they plonked their joshing put-downs an snide one-liners into dull holes.

Then a mobile phone rang and surprised I recognised its sectarian jingle an all went silent until the inspector gasped: 'Fuck. It's the wife.'

'Fuck. It's the wife.'

He said it like he was elsewhere than he should have been,
enjoying guilty pleasures, like he was in a Leith bed and
breakfast wi his subordinate an mistress trying to make
glamorous small talk and big up the empty bog-walk an dullish
smudge o his life, his thinnin hair an elasticated gut which he hid
an was ashamed o. Suddenly he minded me of my grandpa when
I walked into the toilet one morning – saw him brushing his false
teeth er the sink and how angry he got. He slapped me across ma
face. It was the one and only time he hit me as a kid. I don't
know why Grandpa Smeaton plonked into my head then as I
drifted off into a dead kip. Perhaps it was the inspector talking to
his wife. 'I'll be home in time. I ken I'm dog-sitting Bonzo the
night. I'll get a Chinese on the way in.' A laughing duck an black
bean sauce was mooted, an my eyelids felt heavy like lead.

## Four

Security guard's low paid but not if you put the hours in. I got
the job nearly three year ago cos although I share a flat with
three manky layabouts – a dope dealer, a scaffolder and a student
wi nae classes to go to – I'm as smart as a toy soldier just out the
wrapper. Smart uniform, A've added wee touches of my own.
Okay A smoke but I believe in the magic of shoe polish. Whilst
the lads are wading through crisp packets and dead fish suppers
in a flat minus a dust-sucker, lobbing empty beer cans at *Judge
Judy*, I stay in ma room an polish and iron away. The dumb-bells
in the corner have given me a forty-inch chest. I was in the
cadets when I was younger but that fell through cos Mum
wouldny pay for summer camp: 'NO son of mine is going to join
the British Army.' This is my routine jobs: listen to ma sounds,
iron crisp ma company shirts and always being in early for work.
On my day off I go to the library and write my stories. They're
no for anybody else – I guess they are fairly erotic stories but in
them a judgement is prepared also and a world without

deliverance. Cos I always preferred the worst over the better. Better to lie in, mad to rise early an catch the first bus. On a day ticket go round an round until it's time to clock in. Mazing how far you can go on a Greggs sausage roll an a macaroni pie.

That's how I met Gary Glover, being on the shop floor early. You wouldn't believe how early some shoplifters start. The old lady, Mrs Campbell, out of puff because she's wearing three coats, that's her usual routine, putting up a plea for medical attention if you approach too suddenly from amongst the racks of polycottons, and Gary with his fat fingers. They two will cycle by every six months or so. The firm moves us around, shuffling the pack to stay ahead of the chorrers. So they occasionally saunter into my new place with that constipated-about-buying-but-can't-find-the-right-thing look on their faces. Gary's a skinny guy but his hands are puffed up, like he's wearing moon gloves. The blood stays down there due to his wrecked veins. It's what you always end up looking at when talking to Gary Glover. He's not a kid any more and must be quite successful since the gear he wears just keeps getting more cool and sharper every time I see him. I don't nick him, I don't like nicking anybody. Just intervene at the right moment. The first time I caught Gary he had the electronic tab wrapped in tinfoil. I see him on the bus since he lives doon near the park near me. He has an old Alsatian, it's got a whiff of poodle in it. An Aloodle he calls it, a new breed, ken? I do nightclub doors an all sometimes, and I wance let him in when a colleague was for refusing him entry. See when I searched him, feeling how spare he really was, corrugated cardboard for ribs, he said, 'I know you. We've got something in common.' 'I don't have bad breath,' I says. I put my hand in the small of his back and shoved him into the throng thrashing about in the strobe lighting beyond the door.

Now he's standing in a pool o darkness no covered by the CCTV hard by the entrance to Debenhams. Waving to me frae beside a concrete pillar. He's sayin somethin, but I canny hear him cos o the quayside din. I put the cup frae ma flask down on the parapet, clink, an go over to see what he's on about. I'm thinking – do a need handers? A'll call control on my cracklin

radio fur support. I'm just about to press 'call' when I walks
into his airspace an hear what he's sayin clear as a bell: 'Prison
is where the dead men go for their holidays. To prove they're
still alive.' '*Prison*' – the word clangs and bolts cold. A stops an
my finger falls from the radio. This guy has been clued up. An
in ma head a sound that's been following me for months starts
up, sound sweet and dyin, that says life dings heavy than the
heaviness o all things.

'You look like you're about to gee me two inches o cold iron in
my beef, Mr Prentice.' He knows my name which is no surprise.
It's him, here, now, his prison-visitor grin that rings bells. A
shine ma torch in his mug.

His bacon face is all aglow, puffed and swollen. His splattered
nose like a Lorne sausage spread. I know what he's up to. He
wants the inside track. It's a big score tae hae a man on the
inside. Lee doors ajar an exits clear. 'Ner thought you could
outrun the constable for ever, Mr Prentice, did yi?' He laughed
like sheets in a stiff wind, dry and snapping and he'd laugh some
more but my punch to his belly bam – stitched his laugh shut and
a held him up by his lapels as he floated wioot his legs an
wheezed mutterin fucks. Specks o spit on his lips, he looks like
the drowned man. His reek was good as done. Am gonny boot
his arse oot the front door. There was somethin in his piggy eyes
though – calm but more than calm, indolent calm like he was
playin me like a cat's cradle – something's no right. Suddenly
ma feet don't ken where to put themselves. Rebalance. Like A
was expecting a cosh frae oot the dork. I look around. I look
back in time to catch a smile uner his skewed face, uner his
piggy puddle floatin like it went on a moon walk – listening like
a Buddha wid – somethin complicit in that half-hidden smirk,
draws me like a fate wid pull you to its feet, its Buddha toes –
the smile comes wi strings attached. Strings flowing round
corners, down into a manhole. It gave me the shivers to see A
was part o a plan. In the centre o a intricate scheme complex in
its plumbing. A could see Gary in the park, on the bus wi his
Alsatian. A could see him asking me for a light outside Scotmid.
An when I let him off the last time him thankin me for ma
discretion and it'd be guid luck tae us both if A took a bung. 'A

don't take back-handers,' I told him, pushing him out the
emergency exit. Noo he's wheezing freckles o spit on my boots,
as in from the open parapet a cold wind blows, carrying flecks o
snow. Something else about him as I search his pockets for a
clue, somethin about him tuggin at ma recall, familiar like an old
tune, like an unexpected whiff o perfume doon a old close by the
harbour... a sniffed his ruff and fuck me he smells o... a spray o
mirrored images, delicate an veiled like he came an whispered o
his mistress in ma lug. Whispered o her pale-as-milk skin. He
saw in ma face A'd cracked his code an the sparks sunk until all
there was is the grey circles of his eyes. Everythin was turnin
grey. Grey like a haar was smokin frae his bones and him no
more than a pile o clothes on the shingle. He came wi his own
music too which when I looked doon's the melodious tinkle o
water – him was pishin himself noo – aw er oor shoes.

A lifted ma fist but I couldny hit – I drew back ma fist. Then it's
no him being punched in the split mouth but me.

Bash. Thud. Crunch ma nuts. Inspector's got a fist fu o ma hair
and is denting the metal top o the table – smashing ma face off
it. The whole room bounces – the jungle o graffiti bounces an
the gibbons ayont the swastikas shriek silently. He's tellin me,
calmly, how he fancied the Scottish historical novel.
'Waverley's too heavy,' he says. 'I've had the Stewarts.
Tranter's yer man.' Then his knee in ma pit like he stuck a shard
o glass in ma solar and wince as his forearm smash my gullet an
A'm on my knees thinkin 'It's time to pray, time to pray' an A
did, but all A heard was God laughing as the inspector
garrotting me wi ma ain shoelace. He's gruntin like a well-
mired hog – obviously he wasny interested in a confession and
his boot cardboard-boxed ma ribs and my nut met wi the
gurgling pipe and then before the dark the room fills wi angels,
wandering back an forth like they were in God's garden. It's
only when they shift their wings that a great reeving wind blaws
like they're turning the giant leaves o a dark book.

A open my peepers. The room's dark, the neon has finally
packed in. I've been asleep. I must be awake cos there's a
pulsing pain in my heid. Like you wake up after a right
Benidorm bender and you ken you've been in a brawl an all,

cos your knuckles are torn and your lip's swollen and you have
to phone a colleague to find oot wit happened an how it was a
Costa Blanca donkey wit yi shagged – The bolts on the door go
an it swings open and a turn over on my belly to heave mysel
up onto my knees. A'll fuckin get this cunt. I'll grab his ankle an
bite through his tendon. A'll break my teeth on his shin, the
bastard. A'll grab his knackers an fuckin squeeze. But A look up
and it's no the inspector floodin the room wi light but Scarlett
Johansson stonnin there. At first I think this is ma flea-haunted
brain oot o synch – that I'm asleep after all but she reaches out
a hand to pull me up from the floor and I reach out and take it.
My fingers close round hers. Feel her strength as she pulls me
up frae the floor an helps me tae the chair. She's holdin me, my
head by her breasts an gets a glass o water wi rose petals floatin
in it and tries to bring it to my lips an I take the glass from her.
'I'm not hopeless,' A says and we both laugh. Me through
swollen rubber lips and her wi her head thrown back. Then she
leans across me an flicked the switch on the tape recorder and
wi such a sweet voice, in a throaty whisper, telt me about the
day's happenings. How A was tapping ma teeth wi a pen when
several men in suits came into the briefing room and laid their
hands on me yellin, 'You're wanted for questioning, sonny!'
How A threw my Lorne sausage roll at the inspector when he
put it to me in no uncertain terms that A pushed Gary Glover aff
the car-park roof and how A'd set my lawyer a fizzer when A
asked him about his qualifications an whether he was a fish-an-
chips advocate fat on legal aid. She had voices for everybody,
mimicked the desk sergeant an all. Had even voices for herself.
An sweetly tuned me how she was gonny carry me in her erms
to a hotel and wash ma body in the shower an rub my muscles
wi free oils frae the complementary basket. An her lips like ripe
cherry hinging for a kiss. I see ma plans crippled in their
execution laid out like graffiti sprayed. I could see she was
innocent and sweet and I thought though we wander through the
land of pain we don't know the pain we're in – but after many
miles maybe it all comes to an inch o wholeness. I clocks she
has a black eye. I points to it and touchin it she says, 'Nothin a
bit o make-up canny hide.' An she adds mocking me, 'Now will
you lip my tights?' An out the smooth concrete floor like it was

the surface o a pond marvellous lotus flowers rise breaking the surface an their weedy perfume fills the air and crying, sobbin wi pain, I crawl to the wall and wi a broken button frae ma shirt and this gnawing in ma guts I scratch into the plaster: Scarlett Johansson was here.

## Five

Wi a flourish, Inspector produces a transparent plastic bag, waves it in my coupon. My brief sits non-committal. I peers at it – inside is a page torn frae a jotter wi writing on it an much splashed wi what l took to be red wine. 'Gary Glover's suicide note,' says the inspector. 'Found all sort o stuff in his flat, photos o you. Diary o your movement. Seems like he resented you for some reason. Any ideas, sonny, why that might o been the case?' The question hangs in the air like a ping-pong baw defying gravity. The baboons above our heads listen in but nothin's said. I think to myself about how misplaced my kindness might have been in letting Gary Glover go so many times. How he'd clench his fists when I took him down the back stairs to the emergency exit – he never seemed all that happy about me no putting him in a cage.

Then I think I knew what his laughter meant as he stood on the parapet an leant back into the arms o gravity like an infant would. An he threw himself – an aeroplane wi erms for wings and shouted how he'd be ill no more cos he'd be dead. An his laugh seemed to stand on, an trample an kick to fuckin bits the amazed fact that he exists and I thought as he balanced there on the edge how I'd encouraged him to die – not with words but in my heart an why – cos I could smell him like he was close and could see how he mimicked my limp and how he could extract with a grin the evil part in me. I was being lazy when I let him go. Lazy when I didn't run and grab him round the knees. An gobsmacked when the beggar did what I lacked the courage to do and fell and wi a flourish flew with nothing to hide. I stood there in dumb doubt an snowflakes blew in as beyond the parapet the cranes whined. So little to see now I thought – so little to hide.

The inspector fingered the page I'd written with a certain beefy delicacy, sniffing the ink for inconsistency. Then satisfied he asked me to sign my statement – I did so wi a shaking hand. Then he switched the tape recorder off, 'I hope you'll forgive the earlier unpleasantries. I am known to be stern an prompt to anger but I can see you are a moral man and hae a gift and an art.' Then he shovelled another blank page in front of me. The page had a foreboding aspect about its blankness – did the inspector want me to write another statement? My brief put his hand on my arm like he's trying to reassure me that I don't need to write another word, then he clocks his watch.

'It's just this wee story here, what we found in our search o yer flat. It's no finished,' he said looking to ma brief for some support. 'It would be interesting frae a medical perspective. Whilst we wait for the car to fetch you home. I would be disappointed if you didny.' I reached over an picked up the blank page – looked at it. They wanted me to finish *Angels*, bring my wee porn story to an end. I looked at them both and they were nodding in unison. I picked up the pen and it hovered er the blank page in front of me – But where to start? It seemed like a bad dream. I can't stop dreaming, getting several places confused, it makes me forget. Which is the best place to start I thought.

'We've both read the story an as a favour...' the inspector says in an over-droll way. 'Pure unadulterated filth but a wonderful insight into the dysfunctional psychosis of your sociopathic lout, ned, person. I mean person.' My solicitor checked the inspector with a slight hand movement and in silence offered me his own fat Parker pen. After this I would move to another city. After this I would go abroad. After this I would open many new doors and beg for accidents. I grabbed at the page and the point o the Parker sunk into the pristine whiteness. 'It opens your eyes,' the inspector says to my brief. 'I'll never shut them again,' says I, scribbling away.

**Six**

*The following section in brackets can be a voice-over, or said
by the actor or set to music.*

(As I toured, foot-weary, the decaying mansion in which I was
imprisoned I'd occasionally catch sight of myself in a dusty
mirror and recoil, not recognising the dwarf staring back at me
through large soot-rimmed eyes. I'd pass hours in the great hall
doodling drawings with my finger in the dust that coated an
ancient piano... hourglass figures and angelic faces which
seemed to guide my finger and draw themselves. Two words
alone which also wrote themselves over and over again were
'criminal' and 'slave'. In the night I would sometimes find
myself seated here solemnly contemplating the piano's shattered
keys. Occasionally I would awake to find myself playing
discordant sonatas. As if an evil maestro had possession of my
body and was using my fingers to play arrangements full of
mournful anger and deceitful revenge... Bitter chords that
dashed themselves against the stone and seeped into the
threadbare tapestries that hung on the mansion's walls, so that
the mythic animals and heroes cringed at the melodious horror
invading their arcadia. As I played I could see around me the
great tapestries shrivel and waste away. I could smell the threads
rot and hear them snap one by one. What was it I was playing,
bleaching everything whiter than dead coral?

CCCCRRRASSH went the keys like ice detonating.
Mummifying ugliness sounded in the hammers. Wizened lips
*not* kissing went the song. Then sometimes as I played into the
dawn I would hear the crunch of tyres on gravel on the
driveway outside and I would run to the window and look out to
see her, Scarlett, emerge from her Citroën, and she would wave
to me and point down the lawn to where the reeds swayed in a
breeze by the stagnant pond and she would hold up her arms
and laugh as the blackbirds and sparrows an finches warbled

hidden in the trees. Then she'd mouth in an exaggerated way so that I could read her lips: 'Can you keep a secret?' And the dwarf, full of a crazy sorrow, would shake his head and down the window would roll fat rain drops as the Citroën drove back up the drive – its puttering engine fading down the hedgerows.)

I stops writting, nobody says anything, then the inspector nods. Ma brief's nodding too. But I felt they were nodding for totally different reasons. As you do. 'Fair enough,' says the tec. It opens your eyes. 'You're free to go. Your car awaits. A wee freebie tae end the day. Sonny.' Chairs are scraped as aw rise. Bolts pulled an hod onto the rails as A climb the stairs. Fuck yer lift. Smoke soon – the fag I'll hae in the bus shelter. Night ticket.

*The End.*

Nancy Harris
NO ROMANCE
OUR NEW GIRL

Ella Hickson
BOYS
EIGHT
GIFT
PRECIOUS LITTLE TALENT & HOT MESS

Sam Holcroft
COCKROACH
DANCING BEARS
EDGAR & ANNABEL
PINK
WHILE YOU LIE

Liz Lochhead
BLOOD AND ICE
DRACULA *after* Bram Stoker
EDUCATING AGNES ('The School for Wives')
*after* Molière
GOOD THINGS
LIZ LOCHHEAD: FIVE PLAYS
MARY QUEEN OF SCOTS GOT HER HEAD CHOPPED OFF
MEDEA *after* Euripides
MISERYGUTS & TARTUFFE *after* Molière
PERFECT DAYS
THEBANS

Linda McLean
ANY GIVEN DAY
RIDDANCE
SHIMMER
STRANGERS, BABIES

Conor McPherson
DUBLIN CAROL
McPHERSON PLAYS: ONE
McPHERSON PLAYS: TWO
PORT AUTHORITY
THE SEAFARER
SHINING CITY
THE VEIL
THE WEIR

Rona Munro
THE HOUSE OF BERNARDA ALBA *after* Lorca
THE INDIAN BOY
IRON
THE LAST WITCH
LITTLE EAGLES
LONG TIME DEAD
THE MAIDEN STONE
MARY BARTON *after* Gaskell
PANDAS
STRAWBERRIES IN JANUARY
*from* de la Chenelière
YOUR TURN TO CLEAN THE STAIR & FUGUE

Bruce Norris
CLYBOURNE PARK
THE PAIN AND THE ITCH

Ronan O'Donnell
BRAZIL

Lynda Radley
FUTUREPROOF

Andrew Sheridan
WINTERLONG

Ali Taylor
COTTON WOOL
OVERSPILL

Jack Thorne
2ND MAY 1997
BUNNY
STACY & FANNY AND FAGGOT
WHEN YOU CURE ME

Enda Walsh
BEDBOUND & MISTERMAN
DELIRIUM
DISCO PIGS & SUCKING DUBLIN
ENDA WALSH PLAYS: ONE
THE NEW ELECTRIC BALLROOM
PENELOPE
THE SMALL THINGS
THE WALWORTH FARCE

# SCOTTISH COLLECTIONS

## SCOT FREE
*ed. Alastair Cameron*

John Byrne
WRITER'S CRAMP
John Clifford
LOSING VENICE
Anne Marie Di Mambro
THE LETTER BOX
Chris Hannan
ELIZABETH GORDON QUINN
John McKay
DEAD DAD DOG
Rona Munro
SATURDAY AT THE COMMODORE
Tony Roper
THE STEAMIE

## SCOTLAND PLAYS
*ed. Philip Howard*

Catherine Czerkawska
WORMWOOD
Ann Marie Di Mambro
BROTHERS OF THUNDER
Stephen Greenhorn
PASSING PLACES
David Greig
ONE WAY STREET
Liz Lochhead
QUELQUES FLEURS
Linda McLean
ONE GOOD BEATING
Iain Crichton Smith
LAZYBED

**A Nick Hern Book**

*Angels* first published in Great Britain as a paperback original in 2012 by Nick Hern Books Limited, The Glasshouse, 49a Goldhawk Road, London W12 8QP, in association with Blindhorse

*Angels* copyright © 2012 Ronan O'Donnell

Ronan O'Donnell has asserted his right to be identified as the author of this work

Original photo by Nobby Clark
Art design by Jóhanna Helga, www.johannahelga.com
Cover design by Ned Hoste, 2H

Typeset by Nick Hern Books, London
Printed and bound in Great Britain by Mimeo Ltd, Huntingdon, Cambridgeshire PE29 6XX

A CIP catalogue record for this book is available from the British Library

ISBN    978 1 84842 277 3